BLETCHLEY PARK
THE CODE-BREAKERS
OF STATION X

Michael Smith

SHIRE PUBLICATIONS

Published in Great Britain in 2013 by Shire Publications Ltd,
Midland House, West Way, Botley, Oxford OX2 0PH,
United Kingdom.

43-01 21st Street, Suite 220B, Long Island City, NY 11101,
USA.

E-mail: shire@shirebooks.co.uk   www.shirebooks.co.uk

A CIP catalogue record for this book is available from the
British Library.

Shire Library no. 721.   ISBN-13: 978 0 74781 215 9

Michael Smith has asserted his right under the Copyright,
Designs and Patents Act, 1988, to be identified as the
author of this book.

Designed by Tony Truscott Designs, Sussex, UK
and typeset in Perpetua and Gill Sans.

Printed in China through World Print Ltd.

13 14 15 16 17   11 10 9 8 7 6 5 4 3 2

COVER IMAGE
The distinctive half-timbered corner and entrance front of
the Mansion at Bletchley Park.

TITLE PAGE IMAGE
The Mansion at Bletchley Park seen from the lake.

CONTENTS PAGE IMAGE
The code-breakers visited Bletchley Park in August 1938 as
a rehearsal for war using the cover of 'Captain Ridley's
Shooting Party' to disguise their real role.

ACKNOWLEDGEMENTS
The author would like to thank Kelsey Griffin, Gillian
Mason and Claire Urwin at Bletchley Park; Tim Newark,
Russell Butcher and Julie Gribben at Shire Books; and
Jimmy Thirsk and Mary-Lucille Hindmarch for their
assistance in the production of this book.

IMAGE ACKNOWLEDGEMENTS
Alamy, cover image and pages 4–5, 18; Mavis Batey, page
25; Bletchley Park Trust, pages 1, 3, 6–12, 13 (top left
and top right), 14, 16, 17, 20–2, 25, 27 (top), 34, 35, 36,
38, 39 (top), 41, 42, 46, 47, 51, 54; GCHQ (Crown
Copyright, reproduced with kind permission of the
Director), pages 15, 23, 26, 27 (bottom), 28, 29, 30, 31
(top), 33, 37, 43, 44, 45, 48, 49, 50 (bottom), 52; Family
of Wilfred (Bill) Holland, pages 13 (bottom), 31 (bottom),
32, 39 (bottom); Tom Jenkins, page 24 (both); National
Archives, page 50 (top); Den Whitton, page 41.

Shire Publications is supporting the Woodland Trust, the UK's leading woodland conservation charity, by funding the dedication of trees.

CONTENTS

CAPTAIN RIDLEY'S SHOOTING PARTY

BLETCHLEY PARK was bought by Admiral Sir Hugh Sinclair, the head of MI6, in 1938 as a 'war station' for MI6 and its sister code-breaking organisation, the Government Code and Cypher School (GC&CS). Sinclair selected the Park, which was on the edge of the small Buckinghamshire town of Bletchley, because it would be safe from German bombing but still relatively close to London.

The Bletchley Park Mansion. The code-breakers moved to Bletchley Park along with a number of MI6 sections in the middle of August 1939 in anticipation of the outbreak of war.

Shortly after the purchase of the house, the GC&CS code-breakers carried out a brief rehearsal for the anticipated wartime evacuation to 'Station X' as it was now called, not as an indication of secrecy, but simply the tenth of a number of MI6 properties designated with Roman numerals. The practice evacuation was organised by Captain William Ridley, the MI6 administrative officer, as if it were a group of friends spending a weekend in the country, and was given the cover of 'Captain Ridley's Shooting Party'. Meanwhile, workmen moved in to lay a new water main, electricity cables and direct telephone lines to Whitehall.

The mansion itself was an unusual mix of mock-Tudor and Gothic styles, dominated on one side by a large copper dome turned green by exposure to the elements. It looked out over a small lake, rose gardens, a ha-ha and even a maze.

During the inter-war years, GC&CS was staffed largely by the code-breakers who had successfully cracked the German codes during the First World War, with any new recruits restricted to friends or relatives of those 'in the know'. The difficult personalities of some of the code-breakers

led Sinclair, who had overall charge of both MI6 and GC&CS, to believe they should be treated with kid gloves, recalled Josh Cooper, head of the Air Section. 'A man called Fryer threw himself under a train at Sloane Square and [Sinclair] formed the opinion that the work was dangerous and people must not be overstrained.' As a result, Alastair Denniston,

Alastair Denniston, the head of the Government Code and Cypher School, was responsible for the recruitment of the academics and for the relaxed atmosphere which lay at the heart of Bletchley Park's wartime successes.

The Enigma machine was one of a number of cipher machines invented in the wake of the First World War code-breaking successes. This three-rotor version was introduced by the German armed forces in the late 1920s.

the head of GC&CS, ran a very relaxed organisation. The working day began at 10 a.m. and ended at 5.30 p.m., with an hour-and-a-half break for lunch. Barbara Abernethy, who joined GC&CS in August 1937 at the age of sixteen, said: 'Life was very civilised in those days. We stopped for tea and it was brought in by messengers. I was very impressed. It seemed paradise to me.' Sinclair sent his favourite chef from the Savoy Grill to Bletchley with 'Captain Ridley's Shooting Party' to ensure they enjoyed good food. But after a few days of dealing with eccentric code-breakers, the chef himself attempted suicide.

There was very little work on German codes and ciphers before the Second World War, Cooper said. 'It was generally believed that no civilised nation that had once been through the traumatic experience of having its ciphers read would ever allow it to happen again.'

The success of the British code-breakers during the First World War led to the development of cipher machines to foil those trying to read confidential messages. (A cipher represents each letter or figure with another letter or figure, as opposed to a military code, which uses a group of randomly selected letters or figures to represent a word or phrase.)

The German military began using the Enigma machine in the late 1920s. It resembled a small typewriter encased in a wooden box and had a typewriter-style keyboard. On top of the machine was a lampboard with a light for each letter of the alphabet. The operator typed the message into the machine. The action of depressing the key sent an electrical current through the machine and lit up the enciphered letter on the lampboard, which was read off to create the enciphered message. The machine contained three toothed wheels which rotated, changing the encipherment process for each letter typed into the machine. The British rejected Enigma for their own use because in its original form it was relatively easy to break, but the German armed forces added a plugboard, which increased the possible settings to 159 million, million, million, leading them to believe the Enigma ciphers were unbreakable.

'Dilly' Knox, a brilliant code-breaker, who also reconstructed the *Mimes* of the Greek poet Herodas from crumbling pieces of parchment, led the British work against the Enigma ciphers.

The bulk of the GC&CS effort during the inter-war years was aimed at Russian, Italian and, perhaps surprisingly, United States and French codes and ciphers. Only one man worked on the Enigma machine. Alfred Dillwyn ('Dilly') Knox was a brilliant code-breaker and classicist − he had reconstructed the *Mimes* of the Greek poet Herodas from fragments of papyrus found in an Egyptian cave. Knox broke the less complex Enigma machines given by the Germans to their Spanish and Italian allies during the Spanish Civil War, but struggled to get to grips with the version used by the German armed forces until July 1939, when the British began cooperating with the Poles. The Polish mathematician and code-breaker Marian Rejewski had reconstructed the Enigma machine mathematically. While the Polish methods could not cope with the many daily-changing Enigma systems and keys introduced at the start of the war, they gave Knox vital assistance that would help him make the first British break into the German Enigma systems.

The success of the Polish mathematicians also persuaded Denniston to recruit mathematicians to assist Knox. The first, Peter Twinn, who was twenty-three, arrived in February 1939. He and Knox were soon joined by another young mathematician, Alan Turing, who began working part-time with Knox and Twinn. On 15 August 1939, with war seen as inevitable, the code-breakers were ordered to Station X. 'Staff are warned against any conversations regarding the work with other members of the staff whilst in their billets,' they were told. 'This test is to be treated with absolute secrecy.' A total of 110 code-breakers moved to Bletchley, but only thirteen were working on German codes and ciphers, and of these just four – Knox, Turing, Twinn and Tony Kendrick, another of the pre-war classicists – were working on Enigma.

'Dilly' worked on Enigma in 'the Cottage', one of three servants' quarters behind the Bletchley Park mansion. It was here that the first wartime Enigma message was broken in January 1940.

Denniston visited the major universities in the run-up to the war, recruiting mathematicians, linguists and classicists to work at Bletchley. He was later abruptly shoved aside to be replaced by a technocrat. But his recruitment of academics, and the relaxed manner in which he allowed them to work, laid the foundations for the code-breakers' success. 'It would I think be hard to exaggerate the importance for the future development of GC&CS,' Cooper said. 'I have heard some cynics on the permanent staff scoffing at this course; they did not realise that Denniston, for all his diminutive stature, was a bigger man than they.'

Space was limited at Bletchley, with most sections working initially in the Mansion, and there was very little equipment. Edward Green, the Naval Section's office manager, quickly

Leslie Lambert, who was a popular BBC radio personality in the 1930s under the name A. J. Alan, working in the library after the initial move to Bletchley in August 1939.

Joan Wingfield, an Italian linguist, working in the Mansion. The newly built Hut 4, which housed the Naval Section, can be seen in the background.

9

Code-breakers watching a rounders match. Captain Ridley, the MI6 administrator who gave his name to Captain Ridley's Shooting Party, is shown at the far left. Alastair Denniston is standing on the right. Barbara Abernethy is seated, centre, and to her right, with his arms folded, is 'Scrounger' Green.

acquired the nickname 'Scrounger' because of the determined way in which he ensured his code-breakers had everything they needed. Here he describes conditions at the time:

Chaos is a mild term to describe our condition at the outset. We had no furniture, books of reference, maps, atlases, dictionaries or any tools to finish the job. Our difficulties were increased by the fact that our work was so 'hush hush' that we were not able to specify the reason for our importunities. We were expanding at a speed only equalled by rabbits breeding in a warren. I not only had to scrounge tools but if we acquired a typewriter, our next headache was to find a typist to work it. I am told that I once swopped a small and incompetent typist for a large and priceless card index.

Britain was at war but the code-breakers lived a relatively relaxed life. They were billeted in local pubs or people's homes but ate their main meals at Station X. Phoebe Senyard, the Naval Section's head clerk, remembered the 'wonderful lunches' provided for the staff. 'Bowls of fruit, sherry trifles, jellies and cream were on the tables and we had chicken, hams and wonderful beef steak puddings. We certainly could not grumble about our food.'

After lunch, the code-breakers would go out on to the lawn to play rounders. Barbara Abernethy described the scene:

We had a tennis ball and somebody managed to commandeer an old broom handle. If it was a fine day, we'd all say: 'rounders at one o'clock.' We'd all go out and play. Everybody argued about the rules and the dons laid them down, in Latin sometimes. We used trees as bases. 'He got past the deciduous,' one would say. 'No he didn't,' another would argue. 'He was still between the conifer and the deciduous.' That was the way they were.

With more people arriving, wooden huts were erected to house the various sections, which for security reasons took the name of the hut in which they were located. The huts had bare concrete floors coated in red tile paint, windows with blackout curtains, wooden trestle tables, bare light bulbs and inefficient electric or paraffin heaters, or worse, cast-iron coke stoves with metal chimneys going up through the asbestos roof. As winter closed in, the primitive stoves proved inadequate, according to Phoebe Senyard:

Claude Henderson, who was in the Naval Section, working in the Mansion shortly after the arrival at Bletchley.

> They were awful. Long flames would be blown out into the room frightening anyone nearby. Alternatively, the fire would go out and smoke would come billowing forth filling the room with a thick fog, whilst the shivering occupant would be dressed in a thick overcoat, scarf and gloves endeavouring to cope with his work, with all the windows open to let out the smoke.

The drawing room in the Mansion, where staff ate their meals before the construction of the canteen.

BREAKING ENIGMA

THE FIRST British breaks into the German Enigma ciphers were made in January 1940. Knox broke the 'Green' system used by regional military headquarters inside Germany and this was followed by a break into the 'Red' system used by Luftwaffe officers liaising with German troops on the ground. The code-breakers gave different systems the names of colours because progress against each cipher was written on a white-board in different-coloured crayons.

A new section was set up by Gordon Welchman, one of the new young mathematicians, to decipher the Enigma messages. This section, known throughout the war simply as Hut 6, concentrated solely on German army and Luftwaffe Enigma systems. (The more complex naval systems had yet to be broken.) Even where a way was found into the system, Hut 6 still had to break the daily keys. This was done, initially by hand, using a number of methods, the most common of which was a 'crib' — a length of German text expected to appear in the message. Turing and Welchman devised an electrical machine called the Bombe which tested cribs against all the likely settings far more quickly than was possible by hand.

Above: Gordon Welchman, one of the new young academics recruited by Denniston, suggested that the breaking of German army and air force Enigma ciphers be concentrated in one hut, with intelligence reports sent out from a neighbouring hut.

Enigma messages, transmitted in Morse code, were intercepted at armed forces and post office sites across Britain and sent to Hut 6 to be deciphered. They were then passed to the intelligence reporting section in Hut 3, according to Ralph Bennett, one of the intelligence reporters. The two huts 'were linked by a small square wooden tunnel through which a pile of currently available decodes were pushed, as I remember by a broom handle, in a cardboard box, so primitive were things in those days.'

Above left: The increasing number of code-breakers arriving at Bletchley in late 1939 led to the construction of a number of huts to house the rapidly expanding sections.

Left: The huts were very bare inside with minimal comfort and coke stoves that frequently blew back, shrouding the code-breakers in smoke.

Hut 6 (*right*) where the army and air force Enigma ciphers were broken, and behind it the interlinked Hut 3, where the deciphered messages were turned into intelligence reports. This photograph was taken in 2012 before a major renovation programme.

Security was paramount. The messages were disguised as reports from an MI6 spy code-named 'Boniface'. None of the other code-breakers was allowed into Hut 6, Hut 3 or Knox's Enigma Research Section, which was in a cottage behind the mansion and as a result was known simply as 'the Cottage'. 'We knew nothing about Enigma at all until long after the war,' said Julie Lydekker, a member of the Air Section. 'It was a very strange set-up. We were very much in water-tight compartments because of the security so one really only knew one's own sections.'

Hut 6, in particular, fell into complete disrepair before the £7.4 million renovation of Bletchley Park began in 2012.

When Gwen Davies was posted to Station X, as an eighteen-year-old member of the Women's Auxiliary Air Force (WAAF), she was sent to nearby RAF Chicksands. 'I was taken into the administration office [at Chicksands] where there was a driver waiting. He said with perfect seriousness: "Do we blindfold her or use the covered van?" I was shut into the back of a blacked-out van and taken to Bletchley.'

Davies was dumped with her luggage outside the Park gates and told by a young guard that she could not come in because she had no pass.

I was by this time hungry, thirsty and very, very annoyed. 'Look,' I said, 'I don't know where I am, and I don't know what I'm supposed to do.' 'Come to the right place then,' said the guard, 'most of 'em here look as if they didn't know where they was and God knows what

them doing.' I had to sign the Official Secrets Act. I was told that I must never ever say to anyone where I was working and that I must never ever tell anyone about any of the work. You never talked about what you were doing.

The Phoney War came to an end in April 1940, when Germany invaded Denmark and Norway. The 'Yellow' Enigma cipher the Germans used in Norway was relatively easy to break but the fighting was over too soon for it to be of use. By the time the Germans marched into Holland, Belgium and France in May, changes to the Red Enigma meant the code-breakers could no longer read it.

John Herivel, one of the young mathematicians recruited from Cambridge, was determined to find a way back 'into the Red':

I do remember that when I came to Hut 6, we were doing very badly in breaking into the Red. Every evening, when I went back to my digs and when I'd had my supper, I would sit down in front of the fire and put my feet up and think of some method of breaking into the Red. I had this very strong feeling: 'We've got to find a way into the Red again.' I kept thinking about this every evening.

The inside of Hut 6, where German army and air force Enigma ciphers were broken.

Although most of the daily settings were laid down by commanders, the German operators chose the position of the wheels themselves. Herivel realised lazy operators would leave the wheels where they were the previous night or just flick them on a bit. This would show up in the first messages of the day, cutting the possible settings to a mere 17,576. The theory became known as the Herivel Tip. At first it did not work. But on 22 May 1940, Hut 6 code-breakers noted a number of settings very close to each other. They tried various possibilities and managed to break the Red. It was a key moment. Welchman's deputy, Stuart Milner-Barry, recalled:

> I remember most vividly the roars of excitement, the standing on chairs and the waving of order papers which greeted the first breaking of Red by hand in the middle of the Battle of France. This first break into the Red was the greatest event of all because it was not only, in effect, a new key, which is always exciting, but because we did not then know whether our number was up altogether or not.

Below: The winter of 1939–40 saw Bletchley Park covered in snow.

Below right: The lake in front of the Bletchley Park mansion froze over and the code-breakers were able to enjoy skating in their spare time.

Peter Calvocoressi, one of the Hut 3 reporters, recalled that from then on, the Red was always broken, 'usually on the day in question and early in the day. Later in the war, I remember that we in Hut 3 used to get a bit tetchy if Hut 6 had not broken Red by breakfast time.'

Hut 6 and Hut 3 now began working twenty-four hours a day in three eight-hour watches. But Civil Service regulations banned young women from working night shifts alongside men. Putting women on a night shift 'was thought to be not only a strange fad but dangerous to the morals of a mixed community,' Milner-Barry said. 'Indeed, a total of three girls, which was all we required, was thought to be insufficient to ensure the observance of

the proprieties and — presumably on the principle that the men would be overworked by such large numbers – a minimum of six was insisted upon.' As a result, three extra women had to sit through the night shift doing nothing, just to make up the numbers.

Having occupied France, Germany began preparing to invade Britain. Detachments of Home Guards were set up around the United Kingdom. The Bletchley Park Home Guard lacked the discipline of a normal military unit, said Noel Currer-Briggs, an Intelligence Corps officer. 'There were lots of oddballs there. There was one chap from eastern Europe in battledress and a bowler hat, much to the dismay of the sergeant who was trying to make us look smart. It made Dad's Army look like the Coldstream Guards.'

Britain now became the target of German bombers trying to soften the country up for an invasion. The new Prime Minister, Winston Churchill told MPs that with Germany having won the Battle of France, 'the Battle of Britain' was about to begin. The Air Section, led by Cooper, played a key role in collecting intelligence on the Luftwaffe plans by breaking all of its low-level codes and ciphers.

Cooper was one of the more eccentric of the code-breakers. R.V. Jones, head of scientific intelligence, recalled Cooper and two RAF officers interrogating a captured Luftwaffe pilot. The pilot, in immaculate uniform and highly polished jackboots, marched in and came to a halt.

> He clicked his heels together and gave a very smart Nazi salute. The panel was unprepared for this, none more so than Josh who stood up as smartly, gave the Nazi salute and repeated the prisoner's *'Heil Hitler'*. Then realising that he had done the wrong thing, he looked in embarrassment at his colleagues and sat down with such speed that he missed his chair and disappeared completely under the table.

The Battle of Britain gave the Bletchley code-breakers the opportunity for one of their first great contributions to the war. Hut 6 broke a new Enigma cipher, designated 'Brown', used by the Luftwaffe stations in France, which projected the wireless beams that guided German bombers on to their targets. Bletchley was able to predict the precise direction the German bombers would be taking, not only warning the target cities and towns, but also allowing RAF Spitfire and Hurricane fighter aircraft to ambush the German bombers.

Bletchley helped warn Britain's cities when the German bombers would attack during the 1940 Battle of Britain but the code-breakers were not immune themselves and had to help dig their own air-raid shelters.

17

SINK THE *BISMARCK*

B LETCHLEY was expanding fast. One of the earliest new recruits to the
Naval Section, now known as Hut 4, was Harry Hinsley, the son of a
waggoner at a Walsall ironworks. Hinsley had won a scholarship to Cambridge
to study history. The slight, bespectacled young man was an immediate hit
with Phoebe Senyard: 'I can remember showing Harry some of the sorting and
how delighted he seemed when he began to recognise the different types of
signals,' she said. He was put to work alongside Jocelyn Bostock, a young
female civil servant, analysing German naval communications. Senyard said
it was a pleasure dealing with Hinsley 'because he was always interested in
everything and took great pains to find out what it was and why. Those were
very enjoyable days indeed. We were all very happy and cheerful, working
in close cooperation with each other.'

But relations with the Admiralty were less good. Bletchley Park was not
yet seen as a reliable and important source of intelligence. Hinsley spoke
to the Admiralty daily but no one there took any notice of what he said.
'I used a direct telephone line which I had to activate by turning a handle
energetically before speaking,' Hinsley said. 'On this I spoke, a disembodied
voice, to people who had never met me. They rarely took the initiative in
turning the handle to speak to me and they showed little interest in what
I said to them.'

The problem came to a head on 8 June 1940, when the Royal Navy
aircraft carrier HMS *Glorious* and her two destroyers were sunk with the
loss of 1,500 men. Hinsley had warned for weeks that two German
battleships were heading for the North Sea to attack the British ships. 'I was
saying to the duty officer: "For goodness sakes, can't you just persuade them
to send an alert."' But the Admiralty would not do anything on 'inferences
drawn from an untried technique by civilians as yet unknown to its staff'.

The situation finally resolved itself when the Admiralty ignored Hinsley's
warnings that the brand-new German battleship *Bismarck* was leaving the
Baltic to attack the Atlantic convoys bringing vital supplies to Britain.
As Royal Navy ships tracked *Bismarck* waiting to attack her, Hinsley reported

Opposite:
The involvement
of Bletchley Park
in providing
intelligence that
led to the sinking
of the German
battleship *Bismarck*
was the first time
that most of the
code-breakers
realised they were
having an impact
on the war.

Top: Harry Hinsley, the Naval Section traffic analyst whose warnings on *Glorious* and *Bismarck* were ignored by the Admiralty.

Centre: Frank Birch, head of the Naval Section, Hut 4.

Below: The Bungalow, where Turing and Welchman held the key discussions over the construction of the Bombe.

that she was fleeing for the safety of a French port. The Admiralty dismissed this as rubbish, only for a deciphered message to confirm she was heading for the Brittany port of Brest. She was intercepted by British ships and sunk – a major triumph for the British. Because Hinsley's reports were not as secret as the break into Enigma, most of the code-breakers heard about Bletchley's role in the sinking of the *Bismarck*, the first time they knew they were having a real impact on the war.

Malcolm Kennedy, a Japanese interpreter, was in the dining room in the Bletchley Park mansion when news of the sinking came through on the BBC news. 'Spontaneous cheering and clapping broke out from those at lunch when the announcement was made,' he said, 'though some of us had heard the good news slightly before. To give the devil his due, *Bismarck* put up a very good show.'

The sinking of the *Bismarck* was followed by the Royal Navy's destruction of the Italian fleet at the Battle of Matapan

off southern Greece in March 1941, this time as a result of work done in Knox's section. Mavis Lever was nineteen and studying German when war broke out. 'I said I'd train as a nurse. Their response was: "Oh no you don't. You use your German." I thought, great. This is going to be interesting, Mata Hari, seducing Prussian officers. But I don't think my legs or my German were good enough because they sent me to Bletchley.'

On 25 March 1941, Lever broke an Italian Enigma message giving the timing of a planned Italian navy attack on the Royal Navy's Mediterranean fleet. It was passed to Admiral Andrew Cunningham, the British commander, who attacked the Italians first, sinking two battle cruisers and two destroyers. Lever described the moment:

Peter Twinn, the first mathematician recruited by GC&CS. He worked with Turing on naval Enigma and unravelled the wiring of the Enigma circuitry, allowing the creation of the Bombe.

> It was very exciting stuff. There was a great deal of jubilation in the Cottage and Cunningham himself came to visit us. We had a drink and we were in this little cottage and the walls had just been whitewashed. Now this just shows how silly and young and giggly we were. We thought it would be jolly funny if we could talk to Admiral Cunningham and get him to lean against the wet whitewash and go away with a white stern. So that's what we did. It's rather terrible isn't it, these silly young things trying to snare the Admiral.

Naval Enigma was more complex than its army and Luftwaffe equivalents. Alan Turing was obsessed with breaking it, largely because no-one else thought it possible. Turing and Peter Twinn set up the Naval Enigma Section in Hut 8 in June 1940. Their aim was to break *Dolphin*, the Enigma cipher used by the 'Wolf Packs' of U-boats which lay in wait for the Atlantic convoys.

Turing was 'easily the brightest chap in the place', Twinn said. He was also highly eccentric. He cycled to work in a gas mask

Alan Turing, the acclaimed computer genius, whose work at Bletchley focused on the German naval Enigma ciphers and the creation of the Bombe to help break all the Enigma ciphers.

Hut 8, where Alan Turing and Peter Twinn set up the Naval Enigma Section.

to stop pollen sparking off his hayfever, chained his mug to a radiator and bought silver ingots, which he buried as protection against a collapse of the pound, then forgot where they were. The struggle to break into the naval Enigma system depended heavily on captured keys and codes, with Ian Fleming, later the creator of James Bond but then an officer in naval intelligence, helping to coordinate these 'pinches' of German documents. Turing and Twinn finally managed to break *Dolphin* in July 1941, allowing the Admiralty to re-route the convoys around the 'Wolf Packs' while Allied Liberator aircraft picked off individual U-boats.

The Bombes, operated by members of the Women's Royal Naval Service (commonly known as 'Wrens'), were essential to the speedy breaking of the Enigma ciphers. Morag Maclennan joined the Navy at seventeen. She and her colleagues were disappointed to be sent to Bletchley rather than to a port full of sailors:

> We got off at the station and somebody met us and we went up a little gravel path, straight into Hut 11. There were all these machines and you were given a thing called a menu with this strange pattern of letters and figures on it. You had to plait up this machine at the back with these great big leads which had to be plugged into different bits. Then at the front, you had this rack

with rows and rows of drums marked up by colour and you were told what combination of colours you were to put on. You would set them all, press a button and the whole row went round once and then moved the next one on. It took about fifteen minutes for the whole run, stopping at different times, and you recorded the stop and phoned it through and, with any luck, sometimes it was the right one and the code was broken. It was very smelly with the machine oil and really quite noisy. The machine kept clanking around and unless you were very lucky your eight-hour watch would not necessarily produce a good stop that broke a code. Sometimes you might have a good day and two of the jobs you were working on would break a code and that was a great feeling, particularly if it was a naval code.

By the end of the war, there were just under two thousand Bombe operators, of whom 1,676 were Wrens. They had their own unit, HMS *Pembroke V*, and were billeted together at a number of old country houses known as the 'Wrenneries'. The Wrens' arrival improved the code-breakers' social life

The Bombes were located at Bletchley and at outstations such as this one at Eastcote, Middlesex. They were operated by Wrens. Each Bombe bay was named after a country, with individual Bombes given the names of towns in that country.

Some of the 104 relays on the Bombe rebuilt by a team of Bletchley Park volunteers led by John Harper.

Rotors on the reconstructed Bombe at Bletchley Park. The rotors simulated the action of the Enigma machine to try to match streams of clear text that might be in the messages to all possible settings.

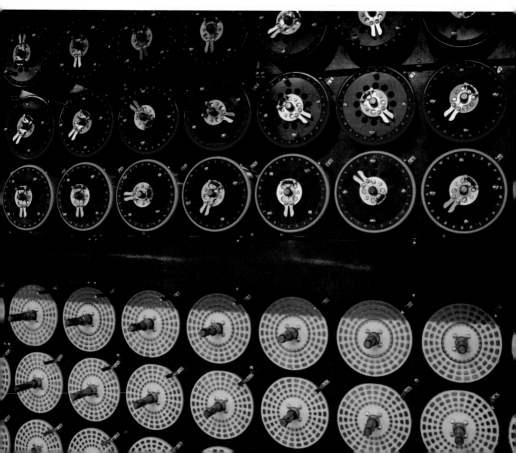

and the Wrenneries became renowned for their dances. Barbara Quirk lived in a Tudor mansion called Crawley Grange, an hour from Bletchley.

Mavis Lever, the leading female code-breaker, whose work on Italian Enigma led to the British defeat of the Italian navy at the Battle of Matapan in March 1941.

> I remember our watch was having a dance in the most glorious ballroom in Crawley Grange, beautiful oak panelling from floor to ceiling, and we were told that we couldn't have any drink. So we got some of the men to bring beer. They brought a mobile bar on a jeep and parked it outside the Wrennery and when the chief officer found out, we were all gated for a month.

Joan Baily was billeted first at Crawley Grange and then at Gayhurst Manor, although she worked at Bletchley Park itself.

> I found the atmosphere rather exciting because we had to try to break these codes and if we didn't get the codes up we knew that somebody had had it. If we were on night shift, we had to sleep during the day of course and I remember they had problems with an RAF aircraft flying low over Gayhurst. We found out afterwards it happened to be because my sister was sunbathing on the roof with nothing on.

The Bombes at Bletchley Park were located in Hut 11.

A CRIME
WITHOUT A NAME

The Hut 6
Registration Room,
where Enigma
messages were
sorted into the
different systems
in use.

GERMAN AND ITALIAN FORCES marched into Yugoslavia and Greece in April 1941. Bletchley predicted the invasions from Luftwaffe preparations reflected in the Red Enigma messages, and heavy movement of German troops and tanks south by rail reported in German Railway Enigma messages. Railway Enigma was broken by John Tiltman, one of the leading code-breakers. Tiltman was so bright he was offered a place at Oxford at the age of thirteen. He won the Military Cross for bravery in the First World War, but was badly wounded and became a military code-breaker, joining GC&CS after the war. Chronic back problems forced him to work standing up at a specially constructed desk. Tiltman always wore his regimental tartan trews,

but had a somewhat casual approach to military discipline. William Filby, a military code-breaker, recalled their first meeting:

John Tiltman, the brilliant military code-breaker who headed the GC&CS Military Section and was in charge of breaking into new ciphers that no-one else at Bletchley could crack.

> My arrival was unforgettable. As I saluted, I stamped the wooden floor in my Army boots and came to attention with another shattering noise. Tiltman turned, looked at my feet, and exclaimed: 'I say old boy. Must you wear those damned boots?' I became the only other rank at Bletchley in battledress and white running shoes, much to the disgust of the adjutant.

During the German invasions of Yugoslavia and Greece, the code-breakers deciphered messages showing a build-up of German troops in Poland, suggesting Hitler was about to turn on his Soviet Allies. On 10 June 1941, Bletchley's Japanese Diplomatic Section translated a message to Tokyo from Oshima Hiroshi, the Japanese ambassador in Berlin, confirming that the invasion of the Soviet Union was imminent. Twelve days later, Hitler launched the aptly named Operation Barbarossa. It provided the most distressing messages the code-breakers would read at any point of the war.

The Hut 6 Traffic Identification Section, which identified the various Enigma radio networks, using traffic analysis techniques.

Reports sent by the SS and Nazi police units mopping up behind the German lines revealed the systematic murder of tens of thousands of Jews. It has been claimed that Bletchley and British Prime Minister Winston Churchill 'covered up' the killings. This is not the case. The reports were passed direct to Churchill and on 24 August 1941, just over five weeks after the first messages were intercepted, he made a BBC broadcast denouncing the 'scores of thousands of executions in cold blood' by German troops. 'Since the Mongol invasions of Europe, there has never been methodical, merciless butchery on such a scale,' Churchill said. 'We are in the presence of a crime without a name.'

Charles Cunningham, one of the code-breakers working on the messages, had taken a short course in German at university.

The Hut 6 team, which controlled interception of Enigma traffic to ensure the most important messages were received clearly.

As a result of that very minimal knowledge the Army posted me to Bletchley Park. On my first day, I saluted this captain and he turned to me and said: 'Excuse me' – not the language normally used by captains to privates – 'Excuse me,' he said. 'What is that noise?' To which I replied: 'That is the air raid siren, sir.' That gives you some kind of an impression of what kind of place Bletchley was; mad people on all sides.

Cunningham deciphered German police messages. He said:

> When you're an individual cryptanalyst just working on the intercepts, you don't have any real overall picture. But there was concern over the concentration camps, which was of course a very inadequate term, and one was aware in the case of stuff coming from these camps that very nasty things indeed were going on. They were run by the SS and they made regular returns of the intake and output and you can guess what the intake was and what the output was. You soon got to have a fairly good idea of what you were dealing with.

The authorities did not just recruit academics as code-breakers. *The Daily Telegraph* ran a crossword competition to provide potential recruits. Stanley Sedgewick's job with a firm of city accountants was classified as a reserved occupation so call-up for military service was deferred. He spent his rail journeys into London solving the *Telegraph* crossword. At the end of 1941, a Mr Gavin, Chairman of the Eccentrics Club, offered to donate £100 to charity if anyone could complete the *Telegraph* puzzle in less than twelve minutes. Sedgewick recalled:

The Hut 6 Decoding Room, where the keys produced by the Bombes were tested to see if they produced plain German text.

This prompted the editor to invite readers wishing to take up this challenge to present themselves at the newspaper's offices in Fleet Street on a Saturday afternoon. I went along to find about thirty other would-be fast solvers. Four of those present completed the puzzle correctly in less than twelve minutes. I was one word short when the twelve-minute bell rang, which was disappointing. Imagine my surprise when several weeks later I received a letter marked 'Confidential' inviting me, as a consequence of taking part in 'The Daily Telegraph Crossword Time Test', to see Colonel [Freddie] Nicholls of the General Staff who 'would very much like to see you on a matter of national importance.' I was told chaps with twisted brains like mine might be suitable for a particular type of contribution to the war effort.

The Hut 6 Machine Room, where, once the day's keys had been broken, Enigma messages were deciphered and typed up ready to be passed to the Hut 3 intelligence reporters.

Sedgewick worked in Josh Cooper's Air Section, on German weather codes. 'The results were used – usually currently – to permit weather forecasts to be made for operational use by Bomber Command,' Sedgewick said. He was unaware until long after the war that they were also used as cribs for Enigma messages.

The rising number of code-breakers led to increased reliance on local households as billets for civilian code-breakers. 'The more people came, the further you had to go,' said Mavis Lever. 'Right over beyond Woburn

The Hut 6 'Duddery', where 'dud' messages that could not be deciphered were checked for errors. Note the Enigma machine (*centre*) used to check results against known keys.

and into Bedfordshire and around Buckinghamshire and a vast system of taking people in and out.'

Each shift was ferried into work and back home again by young female Motor Transport Corps (MTC) volunteers. 'The MTC drivers were really very attractive girls,' said Barbara Abernethy. 'They were usually quite wealthy and had to buy their own uniforms, which were beautifully cut, and they were all pretty. But they worked very, very hard.'

One of the station wagons used to ferry staff to and from their billets, parked in front of the Hut 8 Naval Enigma Section.

The RAF and army personnel were moved into new camps, said Ann Lavell, a member of the Women's Auxiliary Air Force. 'We were hauled out of our billets, many of us wailing and screaming. There was a terrible feeling between the camp authorities and the Bletchley Park people. They couldn't bear it because they didn't know what we did.'

Soldiers and airmen were originally allowed to wear civilian clothes, recalled John Prestwich, a Hut 3 intelligence reporter. 'Then some wretched admiral came down and said: "Where are my Wrens?" And there were these girls in skirts and jumpers and he said: "It's disgraceful. My Wrens should be jumping up, hands down seams of skirts." So we were all made to wear uniform.'

But the informality encouraged by Denniston from the start remained, as Lavell recalled:

> You did have this rather happy atmosphere of tolerance. Very eccentric behaviour was accepted fairly affectionately and I think people worked and lived there who couldn't possibly have worked and lived anywhere else. People who would obviously have been very, very ill at ease in a normal air force camp with its very strict modes of behaviour and discipline were very at ease in Bletchley.

Security remained so tight that when Agatha Christie's spy novel *N or M*, published in November 1941, included a character called Major Bletchley, there was an investigation. Knox, who knew Christie well, invited her to tea and asked her surreptitiously about the name's origins. She explained that she was once stuck at Bletchley station and found the place so boring that she thought it the ideal name for the tiresome old major.

The stable yard, where the station wagons and other motor vehicles were kept and maintained.

The Japanese attack on Pearl Harbor on 7 December 1941 opened a new front, bringing the Americans into the war. Bletchley had shared Japanese decodes with its US Navy and Army counterparts for some time. The United Kingdom had code-breaking outposts in Singapore, which dealt with Japanese naval traffic, and Delhi, covering Japanese army operations, but any new Japanese codes were sent to GC&CS for Tiltman to break. He worked out the Japanese Army's main super-enciphered code – in which messages

US Sergeant George Hurley, one of the United States code-breakers, working in Hut 6.

were first encoded using a codebook and then enciphered for added security – in late 1938. Then, in June 1939, he broke the main Japanese naval super-enciphered code JN25. These successes were shared informally with the Americans.

A more formal agreement between the British and the Americans in December 1940 led to an exchange in which Bletchley revealed how to break Enigma while the Americans reciprocated with their solution to the Japanese diplomatic machine cipher, code-named 'Purple'. As Barbara Abernethy remembers:

> It was early in 1941. Commander Denniston told me: 'There are going to be four Americans who are coming to see me at twelve o'clock tonight. I require you to come in with the sherry. You are not to tell anybody who they are or what they will be doing.' I'd never seen Americans before, except in the films. I just plied them with sherry. It was very exciting and hushed voices.

The Americans were initially treated with suspicion but the mistrust was soon broken down, helped by the fact that the US supply system designated the American code-breakers as independent units, giving them easy access to supplies. 'My office was always very well supplied with sugar,' recalled Joe Eachus, one of the US Navy officers. 'So when I went to another office to ask them to tell me about what they were doing, I would take a cup of sugar with me, which made me a good deal more welcome than I might otherwise have been.'

THE *SHARK* BLACKOUT

THE Christmas dinner of 1941, the last in the mansion, was followed by the first of what became an annual revue involving the many professional actors and musicians at Station X. Pamela Gibson had been on the stage before Birch recruited her for his Naval Section:

The Christmas revues, which included a number of professional actors and musicians working at Bletchley, were the highlight of the busy social calendar.

I spoke German quite well and a rather interfering godmother said she was sure I was doing splendid work entertaining the troops but she knew a girl who had just gone to a very secret place and was doing fascinating work and they needed people with languages. That made me feel I was fiddling while Rome burnt. So I wrote off to the address they sent me and thought no more about it. I had just been offered a part in a play when I got a telegram from Frank Birch asking me to meet him at the Admiralty. He gave

me several tests and said: 'Well, I suppose we could offer you a job.' I said: 'Well you know the stage, what would you do if you were me?' He said: 'The stage can wait, the war can't.' So I went to Bletchley.

The eclectic mix of people at Bletchley fostered an astonishingly varied social life. The Bletchley Park Recreational Club included a drama group, musical and choral societies, as well as bridge, chess, Scottish dancing and fencing sections. Bernard Keefe, who worked on Japanese army air codes, remembered the large number of top-class musicians:

> I was born to a poorish family in Woolwich. My father was a clerk in the local Co-op society, my family descendants of illiterate Irish immigrants who fled the famine in 1849. I shall never forget the impact of arriving in BP; it was a microcosm of the highest intellectual life. There was a lively opera group run by James Robertson, later Music Director of Sadler's Wells – I sang with orchestra for the first time as the Gardener in *The Marriage of Figaro* and the Constable in Vaughan Williams's *Hugh the Drover*. Soon after I arrived, I organised lunch-time concerts in the Assembly Hall outside the main gate. There were many professional musicians – Captain Daniel Jones, the doyen of Welsh composers, Lieutenant Ludovic Stewart, violinist, Jill Medway, a singer, Captain Douglas Jones (later Craig), singer and later company manager at Glyndebourne. There was a choir conducted by Sergeant Herbert Murrill, future Head of Music at the BBC. Working with me was Lieutenant Michael Whewell, bassoonist, and later producer in charge of the BBC Symphony Orchestra.

Until now Bletchley's main customers had been the Admiralty and the RAF. But when British troops defeated the Italian forces in North Africa in early 1941, the code-breakers read messages referring to Luftwaffe escorts for Mediterranean convoys and realised the Germans were about to intervene. Their reports were dismissed by the War Office and Cairo was not informed. A few days later, British troops had their first contact with General Erwin Rommel's Afrika Korps. A secure radio link was set up between Bletchley and its small code-breaking outpost in the Egyptian capital. The code-breakers now broke a Luftwaffe Enigma cipher and the Italian Navy's C38m Hagelin machine cipher, giving the times and routes of the German supply convoys, which enabled the Royal Navy to attack them.

When General Bernard Montgomery took command of the British 8th Army in August 1942, Bletchley provided him with Rommel's plans for an attack on British troops at Alam Halfa, setting up a push by Montgomery that culminated two months

Hut 4 broke the Italian Navy's Hagelin C38m machine cipher, allowing the Royal Navy to pick off the Mediterranean convoys taking supplies to Rommel's troops in North Africa.

Hugh Alexander, one of the most brilliant of the Bletchley Park code-breakers, took over from Turing to lead the attack by the Hut 8 Naval Enigma team on the four-rotor *Shark* Enigma used by German U-boats in the North Atlantic.

The four-rotor *Shark* Enigma cipher machine used by the U-boats patrolling the Atlantic from February 1942 until the end of the war. Despite the fourth rotor, which should have made the code unbreakable, Hut 8 broke it in December 1942.

later in the crucial victory at El Alamein. Within days, a joint American and British force was landing in Morocco, Tunisia and Algeria. Noel Currer-Briggs was in a team sent out from Bletchley to break German low-level ciphers. They set up base in an old Foreign Legion fort. Currer-Briggs recalled:

Fort Sidi M'Cid was built in true Beau Geste tradition on top of a hill above the astonishing gorge which bisects the city of Constantine. It may have looked romantic, but it was the filthiest dump imaginable. One of my most vivid memories is cleaning the primitive latrines. It would be a good punishment if somebody had done something wrong but nobody had. So the adjutant and I said: 'Let's get on and do it', and we started shovelling shit. I can still smell it. I recall with more pleasure, reading Virgil on the battlements. Hardly typical of military life but in the true tradition of BP.

Not all of the social activities at Bletchley were quite as erudite as reading Virgil or listening to classical music, Bernard Keefe recalled. 'There was a great deal of bed-hopping, the odd pregnancy and post-war divorces; all that was much easier for the civilians who lived in outlying villages; we had to make do with the Wrens in whatever nest we could find.'

Diana Russell Clarke, a young WAAF officer, recalled having 'a marvellous time' at Bletchley. 'All these young men, not attached. We had a very gay time going out to pubs for supper together when we were free. A lot of romance went on. The whole thing was absolutely tremendous fun.'

Aside from the fighting in North Africa, it was the Battle of the Atlantic which dominated Bletchley's work throughout 1942. On 1 February, the U-boats introduced a new Enigma machine with a fourth wheel, making their messages unreadable. Bletchley code-named the new machine *Shark*. The vital intelligence the Admiralty had been using to re-route the Atlantic convoys around the 'Wolf Packs' disappeared for ten months, a period known to the code-breakers as 'the *Shark* Blackout'. 'It was a grim time,' recalled Shaun Wylie, who worked in Hut 8. 'There was a lot of pressure. We realised our work meant lives.'

Hugh Alexander, a former United Kingdom chess champion, took over from Turing as head of Hut 8 and led the attempts to break *Shark*. Fortunately, during the first half of 1942, the U-boats concentrated on the American coastline. They resumed attacks on the Atlantic convoys in August with eighty-six U-boats, four times as many as when *Shark* was introduced, sinking eleven ships in one attack.

During August and September 1942, the U-boats located twenty-one of the sixty-three convoys, sinking forty-three ships. Allied losses climbed sharply and towards the end of November, with the number of ships lost that month close to the hundred mark, the Admiralty demanded that Hut 8 pay 'a little more attention' to the U-boat cipher. In a tersely worded memorandum, it complained that the U-boat campaign was 'the only campaign which Bletchley Park are not at present influencing to any marked extent and it is the only one in which the war can be lost unless BP do help.'

Female Hollerith operators punching data cards in the 'Freebornery' Machine Room. The Hollerith data-processing machines run by Frederic Freeborn were invaluable in breaking all of the main ciphers read at Bletchley Park.

A Hollerith punch card. The data recorded on these cards was a vital aid to the code-breakers.

Two days later, two German codebooks arrived at Bletchley. They had been recovered from the U-559, scuttled by its crew after an attack by the British destroyer HMS *Petard* off Egypt on 30 October 1942. The *Petard*'s first officer, Lieutenant Anthony Fasson, and Able-Seaman Colin Grazier swam to the submarine and passed the codebooks out to sixteen-year-old Naafi boy Tommy Brown. Fasson and Grazier went down with the U-559 and were awarded the George Cross posthumously. Brown received the George Medal. Their heroism was vital in helping to end the blackout.

The codebooks were for lower grade German naval codes but they allowed the code-breakers to break messages that were also sent on the *Shark* circuits, providing 'cribs' that, with luck, would give Hut 8 a way in.

Wylie took over the code-breaking shift in Hut 8 at midnight on 12 December 1942. They worked through the night trying to match the messages broken with the codebooks against Enigma messages, but without luck. But next morning, they made the vital breakthrough. Wylie was eating breakfast in the newly constructed canteen when he heard the news. 'Somebody rushed in and said: "We're back into the U-boats",' Wylie recalled. 'It was a great moment. The excitement was terrific. Relief too.' Within hours, the Admiralty was once more routing the Atlantic convoys around the 'Wolf Packs'.

The new canteen could hold a thousand people at a single sitting. Across the Park new concrete blocks were constructed throughout 1942 and into

Blocks A and B, the first of the new concrete blocks – much more amenable than the smoke-filled huts – were built during the summer of 1942.

1943. 'We moved from Hut 4 which we loved, into a horrible concrete building,' said Sarah Norton, a Wren who worked in Birch's Naval Section.

Code-breakers relaxing behind one of the huts.

To be totally perverse, we insisted on still calling the new block Hut 4. It had a long corridor which ended in a T-junction. One afternoon, we decided to give Jean Campbell-Harris, later Baroness Trumpington, a ride in a laundry basket on wheels that was normally used to move secret files. We launched it down the long corridor where it gathered momentum by the second. To our horror, at the T-junction, Jean suddenly disappeared, basket and all, through some double-swing doors crashing to a halt in the men's toilets. A serious reprimand was administered and our watches changed so we were distributed among a more sober group. But this fortunately did not last long.

The huts and the new blocks that crowded Bletchley Park from 1943 onwards viewed from the Mansion: Block G in the distance (*far right*), Block F (*far left*); huts 6 and 3 (*centre right*).

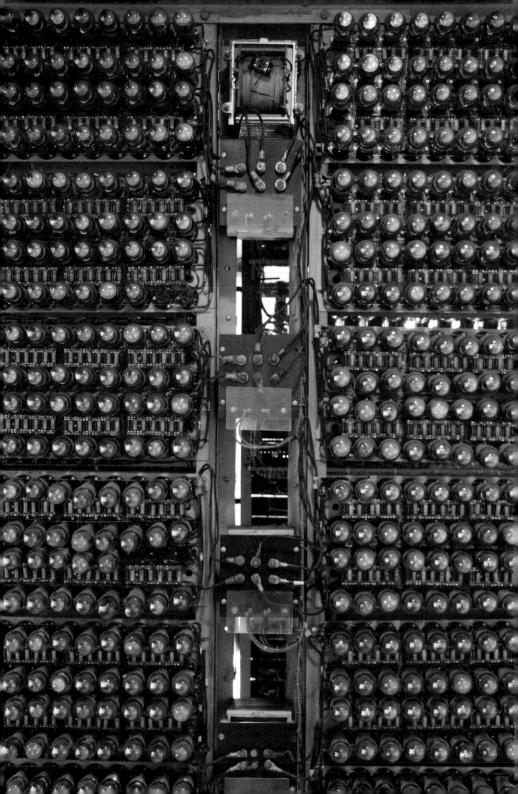

COLOSSUS: THE WORLD'S FIRST PROGRAMMABLE COMPUTER

THE ALLIED INVASION of Italy in July 1943 and the swift Italian surrender left Bletchley uncertain whether Hitler would retreat to the Alps, saving men and material for the Allied invasion of Europe, or fight every inch of the way. The answer came not from the breaking of Enigma, but from the Lorenz SZ40 enciphered teleprinter system. This was introduced in 1940 for the highest-level German communications between Berlin and the commanders of the various military fronts. It had twelve wheels: ten to encipher the message (paired in two separate rows of five) and two drive wheels. The movement of the second row of wheels was highly complex, making the cipher extraordinarily difficult to break. But in late 1941, by a combination of genius and luck, it was broken by John Tiltman and one of the young Cambridge mathematicians. Bill Tutte had been rejected by Turing for Hut 8 but Tiltman spotted his ability. There were a number of different German teleprinter cipher machines, to which the code-breakers gave the collective code name *Fish*. But they concentrated on the German Army's Lorenz system, code-named *Tunny*, because it produced the best intelligence. This included messages between Berlin and the headquarters of Field Marshal Albert Kesselring, the German commander in Italy, confirming that Hitler had decided that German troops would defend Italy to the last.

'This was the strategic prize of the greatest moment,' said Ralph Bennett. 'It enabled the Allies to design the Italian campaign to draw maximum advantage from the willingness Hitler thus displayed to drain away his resources.'

The breaking of the *Tunny* cipher took place in two stages. The first determined the setting of the first row of five wheels, which rotated regularly. This was carried out by a section known as the

Bill Tutte, who with the assistance of John Tiltman broke the first *Tunny* message read at Bletchley Park.

Max Newman, Turing's tutor at Cambridge, who led 'the Newmanry', one of two teams working on the *Tunny* enciphered teleprinter messages, and who first suggested creating a computer to help to break the ciphers.

Ralph Tester, the army officer who led the 'Testery' team which deciphered the *Tunny* messages by hand when the preliminary calculations had been carried out by the Newmanry.

Tommy Flowers, the head of the Post Office research department at Dollis Hill, north London, who created Colossus, the world's first semi-programmable electronic digital computer.

Newmanry after its head, Max Newman, who had been Turing's tutor at Cambridge. The second section, led by Ralph Tester and called the Testery, used the stream of letters produced by breaking the setting of the first row of wheels to decipher the actual messages by hand.

It was Newman who posed the question which led to Turing's groundbreaking treatise 'On Computable Numbers with an Application to the *Entscheidungsproblem*', now seen as predicting the modern computer. Newman believed the work carried out in the Newmanry could be done by such a machine. The result was the construction by Post Office engineer Tommy Flowers of the Colossus computer, the world's first electronic digital computer. Colossus did not break the messages. This still had to be done by hand. But it made the process of breaking the setting of the first row of wheels far quicker. According to Flowers:

The purpose of the Colossus was to find out what the positions of the wheels were at the beginning of the message. It did that by trying all the possible combinations and there were billions of them. It tried all the combinations, which processing at five thousand characters a second could be done in about half an hour. So then having found the starting positions of the cipher wheels you could decode the message.

The computers were operated by Wrens. Odette Murray was one of those working on Colossus. 'I was given instructions by whoever was in charge at the time and, not having the remotest idea what I was doing, worked with a slide-rule producing a lot of figures and gave the result to the next person who gave it to the next person and eventually it was run [through Colossus] on a tape.' Shaun Wylie, her future husband, had just been transferred into the Newmanry from Hut 8 when she arrived. She recalled:

All the Wrens were swooning about Shaun Wylie. They thought he was absolutely wonderful: 'Oh, Mr Wylie this. Oh, Mr Wylie that.' I didn't think much of him. I couldn't see what they saw in him. However, he thought something of me. He tried to explain what my contribution had been in a successful thing. I just didn't understand. I'm not a mathematician, I'm not a linguist. I'm just somebody who's given instructions and does little funny calculations with a slide-rule and bingo. A few days later a smiling Shaun comes in. I don't know what my contribution is but okay, satisfactory.

Following the surrender of Italy, many of the people working on Italian codes and ciphers were switched to Japanese. Two Japanese language courses were set up, one by Tiltman in Bedford and the other by Josh Cooper's Air Section, which needed linguists capable of translating the radio conversations of Japanese pilots. Cooper's training method was described by Tiltman as 'a rather more tricky experiment' than his own:

> What the RAF needed was interpreters who could read air-to-ground and air-to-air conversations. For this purpose my counterpart in the Air Section, Cooper, started an intensive eleven-week course at which the students were bombarded incessantly with Japanese phonograph records, ringing the changes on a very limited vocabulary. The course was directed, not by a Japanese linguist, but by a phonetics expert. I remember taking a US Army Japanese interpreter Colonel Svensson round the course. Stunned by the volume of sound in every room, Svensson mildly asked the Director whether all the students made the grade and the reply he received was: 'After the fifth week, they're either carried away screaming or they're Nipponified'.

Robinson, the first machine built to help break the *Tunny* ciphers, named after Heath Robinson, the artist who created paintings of fantastic machines. It was unreliable and was replaced by Colossus.

Colossus 6,
the sixth version
of the Colossus
computer used
by the Newmanry
to break
the settings of
the first set
of wheels on the
SZ42 *Tunny* cipher.

Gladys Sweetland, a young corporal in the women's army, the women's Auxiliary Territorial Service (ATS), was recruited to work on Japanese army codes:

It was really rather weird. I was taken into a hut and introduced to what I was supposed to do. Teleprinter sheets of coded messages were handed to me and I had to copy each message out in different coloured inks across one line

Colossus 10 being
operated by two
Wrens, Dorothy
du Boisson (*left*)
and Elsie Booker.

on large sheets of graph paper. Each message was marked with a sign to indicate which colour ink I should use. I know it sounds ridiculous but we never asked what they did with the sheets of messages. It was all so secret. Even with the other girls in the ATS we only ever asked: 'Where do you work?' And they'd say: 'Oh, Hut 6' or 'Block F' or whatever. We never asked each other what we actually did.

Bletchley Park was a wonderful location and sometimes we just sat in the grounds in fine weather for our break. There was an assembly hall just outside and it was there I got my love for opera and ballet because I saw the D'Oyly Carte touring company and the Ballet Rambert. There were also discussion groups where people would play classical music records and then explain the merits of the various pieces. I shall never forget the comradeship and meeting all those different types of people who were there. I never thought, leaving school at fourteen and a half, that I would be able to have a proper conversation with a university professor.

The Tape Machine Room in the Newmanry, where Wrens prepared the paper teleprinter tapes that would be run through the Colossus computer to break the settings of the first set of wheels used to create the *Tunny* ciphers.

After the victories in the Atlantic, North Africa and Italy, Christmas 1943 was a time of real celebration, particularly in Hut 4, where Birch ensured

that despite rationing his staff had an excellent Christmas lunch. Phoebe Senyard recalled:

> We toasted the Naval Section and anything else that came into our heads. It was great fun and by the time we went into the room where the luncheon was served, we were prepared for almost anything but not for the wonderful sight which met our eyes. The tables were positively groaning with Christmas fare. They were arranged in a T-shape. The top of the T was loaded with turkey, geese, and chicken, while the table down the centre at which we all sat was decorated with game pie, and fruit salad, cheese and various other dishes. We set to and thoroughly enjoyed ourselves and I was still beaming by the end of the day.

Pat Wright was working in Hut 8 on Christmas Day deciphering Enigma messages, and recalled returning to her billet at the end of the shift:

The recreated Colossus computer, rebuilt in the 1990s by former MI5 technical expert Tony Sale and a team of volunteers.

> It was the first house I had come across that had a toilet in the garden and I had spent five minutes of my first evening there with my toilet bag touring around looking for the bathroom. But Mrs Tomlin was very good to me. She had an engine-driver husband and a fireman son and she always had food on the table. She was a very capable woman with a range of language I had never encountered before. I had been brought up fairly strictly and she used words I hardly knew the meaning of. I was working Christmas day and so I finished work at four o'clock and went back to my billet. Christmas dinner was over but she said: 'Hello duck, saved you a bit of Christmas pudding. Here you are, this'll make your shit black.' I didn't know whether to laugh or what to do. So I said thank you very much and ate it.

D-DAY
AND DOUBLE CROSS

THE COLOSSUS COMPUTER worked well but Tommy Flowers was already building an even faster version. Bletchley told him that if it was not ready by early June 1945 it would be no use at all, which he rightly assumed to mean that the D-Day invasion would take place then. 'We worked flat out for four months and met the deadline, but only just,' Flowers recalled. 'I was at Bletchley Park on that historic day [D-Day, 6 June 1944] and had been since the morning of the previous day, dealing with the last few difficulties. The machine was fully ready for service for the first time during the small hours of 1 June.'

The code-breakers provided Allied planners with a comprehensive picture of the German defences and their plans to counter the Allied invasion. The Japanese Ambassador, Oshima Hiroshi, toured northern France sending a highly detailed picture of the German defences back to Tokyo. He reported that the troops in France would be reinforced by three SS armoured divisions and, critically for Allied deception plans, that the Calais region was seen as the most likely site of an Allied landing. The Japanese Military Attaché, whose cipher had been broken by Tiltman in 1942, made his own tour of the defences, sending an even more comprehensive account of every building and installation, detailing everything from the heaviest artillery battery to the smallest collection of flame-throwers. Anything missed by these two accounts was filled in by the Japanese Naval Attaché in Berlin, whose report was also read at Bletchley.

The *Abwehr* Enigma cipher, possibly the most complex of all the Enigma ciphers read at Bletchley, was broken by Dilly Knox in December 1941.

The Sixta 'DF Plotting Room'. British intercept sites used direction-finding equipment to plot a bearing to the German radio station. The bearings from two or more sites were plotted on the map to find the location of the station.

Sixta, the section which analysed traffic to find new clues about the various Enigma networks, often producing vital intelligence.

The extent of the intelligence provided by the code-breakers ahead of D-Day was extraordinary. In March, assisted by the arrival of the first Colossus, they broke into the *Fish*-enciphered teleprinter link between Field Marshal Gerd von Rundstedt, the German commander in France, and Berlin. This link, code-named *Jellyfish* by Bletchley, carried all of von Rundstedt's communications with Hitler and confirmed that the Germans expected the Allies' main force to land at Calais rather than in Normandy.

The Hut 6 Fusion Room, where deciphered Enigma messages and traffic analysis carried out by Sixta were 'fused' to put together a complete intelligence picture.

The confirmation from Bletchley that the Germans believed the Allies would land in the Pas de Calais was central to the *Fortitude South* deception plan worked out to protect the Normandy landings. The presence of 1.4 million German troops in France meant the invasion was far from certain to succeed. If the Allies were to get a foothold in Normandy, it was vital that the Germans kept most of their forces in the Calais area.

From the start of the war, British intelligence had captured every spy sent to Britain by the German secret service, the *Abwehr*, and had been using them to feed false information to German commanders. The problem for the British officers controlling the Double Cross system, as it was known, was that they could not be certain the Germans believed these false reports. Messages between the *Abwehr* agent-runners and Germany were enciphered on a highly complex Enigma machine. Not only did it have four wheels; they rotated far more often than on the standard machine, making it much more difficult to crack. Hut 6 could not break it but Dilly Knox was convinced he could and on 8 December 1941, assisted by the female code-breakers Margaret Rock and Mavis Lever, he succeeded. From that point on, the Double Cross controllers knew the Germans believed the false intelligence.

This allowed the British to take the Double Cross deception one stage further in the run-up to D-Day, supplying coordinated intelligence from all the double agents to create a completely false picture of a fictitious First United States Army Group, based in south-east England, that would lead the Allied invasion of the Pas de Calais; with the Normandy landings simply a feint to draw German attention away from Calais area. The *Fortitude*

Juan Pujol García, code-named 'Garbo', the Spanish double agent who played the key role in the D-Day 'Double Cross' deception with his messages tracked by Bletchley from the *Abwehr* Enigma cipher.

Women often achieved far more equality at Bletchley than was normal elsewhere. This female code-breaker is in charge of the Hut 6 Operations Room during her shift or 'watch'.

South deception plan would ensure the Germans kept most of their forces in Calais rather than Normandy.

The most important of the Double Cross agents used in the deception was a Spaniard called Juan Pujol García, code-named 'Garbo'. He claimed in his reports to the Germans to be running a network of twenty-seven agents across the United Kingdom, including a Swiss businessman in Bootle who reported 'drunken orgies and slack morals in amusement centres' in Liverpool, and a Venezuelan in Glasgow who claimed Clydeside dockers would 'do anything for a litre of wine'. When the Swiss businessman died of cancer, his widow took his place. The Venezuelan also ran agents in Scotland, one of them a communist who thought he was spying for Moscow. Garbo's mistress, a secretary in the War Cabinet, slept with army officers to gather valuable pillow talk. Garbo also had a network of agents in Wales, mostly Welsh Nationalists, who were led by 'a thoroughly undesirable character' who worked purely for money. None of these agents actually existed. Garbo's claims were so incredible that it would have been impossible to imagine that the Germans believed anything he said, if it were not for Bletchley's ability to read the messages enciphered on the *Abwehr* Enigma.

In the early hours of D-Day, 6 June 1944, as Allied troops poured across the English Channel, Garbo tried repeatedly to warn Berlin that they were on their way to Normandy. It was deliberately too late for the Germans to do anything about it, but ensured they still saw Garbo as their most reliable spy.

Three days later, with Allied forces struggling to break out of their bridgehead, and two German armoured divisions on their way to Normandy, Garbo sent his most important message. His agents were reporting troops massed in ports in East Anglia and Kent, he said. The Normandy landings were a diversion. The real landings were to be in Calais as the Germans had always believed. Garbo's warning went straight to Hitler, who ordered the two armoured divisions back to Calais to defend against what he expected to be the main invasion thrust. This ensured the success of the Allied invasion. Had the two divisions continued to Normandy, the Allies might well have been thrown back into the sea.

The Fortitude South deception plan would not have been possible if Knox had not broken *Abwehr* Enigma. Sadly, he did not live to see the result of what was by far the most important of his, quite possibly of Bletchley's, many code-breaking successes; when Knox broke the *Abwehr* Enigma in December 1941, he was already suffering from terminal cancer. He died in February 1943, sixteen months before D-Day.

The contribution made by the code-breakers to the Allied victory is truly incalculable. Bletchley Park did not win the war – no single organisation could make that claim – but its contribution to the defeat of Hitler was enormous.

Block D, which housed the Enigma processing sections, Hut 6, Hut 3 and Hut 8, together with Sixta, from November 1943 until the end of the war.

The extent of its effect on the victories in the Battle of Britain, the Battle of the Atlantic, the war in North Africa and at D-Day is impossible to calculate. But such was the code-breakers' commitment to secrecy that their achievements remained unknown and unrecognised until the mid-1970s when the then British Foreign Secretary David Owen released them from their wartime pledge of secrecy. Even then, it was so deeply ingrained that many found it impossible to open up to friends and relatives who might still have thought they had spent the war in a 'cushy billet' playing little or no part in the Allied victory.

Olive Humble, a young civil servant, was one of the thousands of young women from ordinary working-class backgrounds working at Bletchley. At the end of the war, she was ordered by a senior naval officer to 'keep my mouth shut for all time, and threatened with thirty years or the firing squad if I went off the straight and narrow.' She adds:

> One thing I regret deeply. I was an only child. On my first day home my father at dinner said: 'What do you do at the Foreign Office?' I replied: 'I cannot tell you. Sorry, please don't ask me again' – and he didn't, nor did my mother at any time. She died in the early 1960s and he in 1976, before I realised the silence had been lifted.

It is estimated that the breaking of the German Enigma and Lorenz ciphers cut around two years off the war, saving countless lives. But the impact of Bletchley Park's work on Japanese and Italian ciphers is too often forgotten. Just as importantly, it was the birthplace of the modern computer, Colossus being the world's first programmable digital electronic computer. No wonder George Steiner, the American philosopher, described Bletchley Park as 'the single greatest achievement of Britain during 1939–45, perhaps during the [twentieth] century as a whole.'

The Bletchley reports were sent out using highly secure cipher machines. The Rockex cipher machine seen in use here was developed by the MI6 New York Rockefeller Plaza office (hence its name) for use by the intelligence services.

FURTHER READING

Batey, Mavis. *Dilly: The Man Who Broke Enigma*. Biteback, 2009.

Bennett, Ralph. *Ultra and Mediterranean Strategy 1941–1945*. Faber & Faber, 2009.

Bennett, Ralph. *Ultra in the West: The Normandy Campaign 1944–1945*. Faber and Faber, 2009.

Birch, Frank, and Jackson, J. (editors). *The Official History of British Sigint*. Military Press, 2009.

Briggs, Asa. *Secret Days: Code-breaking in Bletchley Park: A Memoir of Hut Six and the Enigma Machine*. Frontline, 2011.

Budiansky, Stephen. *Battle of Wits: The Complete Story of Code-breaking in World War II*. Simon & Schuster, 2002.

Conyers Nesbit, Roy. *Ultra Versus U-Boats: Enigma Decrypts in the National Archives*. Pen & Sword, 2008.

Copeland, B. Jack, and others. *Colossus: The Secrets of Bletchley Park's Code-breaking Computers*. Oxford University Press, 2010.

Denniston, Robin. *Thirty Secret Years: A.G. Denniston's Work in Signals Intelligence 1914–1944*. Polperro, 2007.

Erskine, Ralph, and Smith, Michael (editors). *The Bletchley Park Code-breakers*. Biteback, 2011.

Gannon, Paul. *Colossus: Bletchley Park's Greatest Secret*. Atlantic, 2007.

Grey, Christopher. *Decoding Organization: Bletchley Park, Code-breaking and Organization Studies*. Cambridge University Press, 2012.

Herivel, John. *Herivelismus and the German Military Enigma*. M. & M. Baldwin, 2008.

Jackson, John (editor). *The Secret War of Hut 3: The First Full Story of How Intelligence from Enigma Signals Decoded at Bletchley Park Was Used During World War Two*. Military Press, 2002.

Kahn, David. *The Code-breakers: The Comprehensive History of Secret Communication from Ancient Times to the Internet*. Simon & Schuster, 1997.

Kahn, David. *Seizing the Enigma: Race to Break the German U-boat Codes. 1939–43*. US Naval Institute Press, 2012.

Hill, Marion. *Bletchley Park People*. History Press, 2004.

Hinsley, F. H. *British Intelligence in the Second World War* (Abridged). TSO, 1993.

Hinsley, F. H. and Stripp, Alan. *Code-breakers: The Inside Story of Bletchley Park*. Oxford University Press, 2001.

Hodges, Andrew. *Alan Turing: The Enigma*. Vintage, 1992.

Lewin, Ronald. *Ultra Goes to War: The Secret Story*. Penguin, 2001.

McKay, Sinclair. *The Secret Life of Bletchley Park*. Aurum, 2010.

Parrish, Thomas. *The Ultra Americans: The U.S. Role in Breaking the Nazi Codes*. Stein & Day, 1986.

Piper, Fred, and Murphy, Sean. *Cryptography: A Very Short Introduction*. Oxford University Press, 2002.

Sebag-Montefiore, Hugh. *Enigma: The Battle for the Code*. Phoenix, 2004.

Smith, Michael. *Station X: The Code-breakers of Bletchley Park*. Pan, 2004.

Smith, Michael. *The Emperor's Codes: Bletchley Park's Role in Breaking Japan's Secret Ciphers*. Dialogue / Biteback, 2010.

Smith, Michael. *The Secrets of Station X: How the Bletchley Park Codebreakers Helped Win the War*. Biteback, 2011.

Smith, Michael. *Britain's Secret War 1939–1945*. Andre Deutsch, 2011.

Stripp, Alan. *Codebreaker in the Far East*. Routledge / Cass, 2004.

Stubbington, John. *Kept in the Dark, The Denial to Bomber Command of Vital Ultra and Other Intelligence Information during World War II*. Pen & Sword, 2010.

Thirsk, James. *Bletchley Park: An Inmate's Story*. Gallago, 2008.

Watkins, Gwen. *Cracking the Luftwaffe Codes: The Secrets of Bletchley Park*. Greenhill, 2006.

Welchman, Gordon. *The Hut Six Story: Breaking the Enigma Codes*. M. & M. Baldwin, 1997.

Winterbotham, Frederick W. *The Ultra Secret: The Inside Story of Operation Ultra*. Orion, 2000.

Skating on the lake during time between shifts.

PLACES TO VISIT

BLETCHLEY PARK

Bletchley Park is close to the railway station in Bletchley in Buckinghamshire. The Mansion and many of the key buildings can be visited, including the Cottage where Dilly Knox broke the first German wartime Enigma message; Hut 6, where German army and Luftwaffe Enigma was broken; and Hut 3, where the message content was turned into intelligence reports. There is a comprehensive museum, including a number of cipher machines. There are also reconstructions of the Colossus computer and the Bombe, the electrical machine used to break the Enigma messages.

Telephone: 01908 640404. Website: www.bletchleypark.org.uk

THE NATIONAL ARCHIVES

The National Archives at Kew, in south-west London, hold an extensive collection of documents on Bletchley Park, including the internal histories of all the main sections and all of the messages sent direct to Churchill. These include a series of special reports produced for Churchill on the massacres of Jews by SS and German police troops on the eastern front in 1941 on which the British Prime Minister circled in red ink the precise numbers of those killed ahead of a speech in which he denounced the killings as 'a crime without a name'. All of these documents are accessible to any visiting member of the public.

Telephone: 0208 876 3444. Website: www.nationalarchives.gov.uk/visit/

INDEX